Westward Expansion Before the Civil War

Reader

Core Knowledge®

ISBN: 978-1-68380-223-5

Westward Expansion Before the Civil War

Table of Contents

Westward Expansion Before the Civil War
Reader
Core Knowledge History and Geography™

Chapter 1
Daniel Boone

On the Move With travel so difficult in the 1700s, you would expect most people to stay close to home. Most did, never going more than a few miles from their farm or village. But there were some daring Americans who, despite all the hardships of travel, set off in search of new beginnings.

The Big Question
....
What were some of the reasons why so many people wanted to move west?

Many people traveled by wagon across hundreds, even thousands, of miles as they moved west.

What drove these people on, despite all the obstacles of travel? Some were in search of adventure. Some sought new, rich land for farming. Still others simply wanted a place where they could start over. And so they moved west. They came to be known as **pioneers**. In lands unknown to them, they learned to be **self-reliant**.

Vocabulary

pioneer, n. one of the first people to settle in a region

self-reliant, adj. needing no help from other people

Moving West

Hunters and trappers first led the way into the lesser-known areas, and one of the most famous was Daniel Boone. Born and raised near the edge of Pennsylvania's wilderness, Daniel received his first rifle when he was twelve years old. He became a skilled rifleman. Daniel loved to spend time with the Native Americans who lived nearby, and they taught him how to hunt and trap forest animals.

When Daniel was sixteen, his family moved to North Carolina, along the eastern side of the Appalachian Mountains. At that time, a small number of settlers lived in the wilderness there. Daniel began spending several months each year in the woods, with only his rifle for company. He hunted for his food and slept under the stars. He earned money by selling the furs of the animals he killed. For some, the fur trade was a fairly profitable business.

Daniel eventually grew up, got married, had a family, and started a farm. But the wilderness had a hold on Daniel Boone's imagination and would not let go. Every autumn after harvesting the crops, he headed back to the forest. He'd live there until the spring, when it was time to plant the next year's crops.

The Wilderness Trail

The western **frontier** marked the end of the area settled by Americans and the beginning of unknown land, or wilderness. By the 1760s, the frontier reached the Appalachian Mountains. But there it stopped. The mountains formed a physical

Vocabulary

frontier, n. where newly settled areas meet unsettled, but not necessarily uninhabited, areas

barrier to the West. In addition, the British issued an order that prevented settlers from moving beyond the mountain range. They did this to prevent possible conflicts with Native Americans who lived on these lands.

For years, Daniel Boone had heard other hunters and traders tell of a rich land on the other side of the Appalachians. They said an old Native American trail called the Warrior's Path led the way. Although Boone searched for the trail several times, he failed to find it.

Finally, in 1769, Boone and a group of five companions found what they were looking for. The Warrior's Path led them into a gap, or narrow pass, between the mountains. Arriving at the other end of the pass, Boone and his friends found themselves on the western side of the Appalachians. There, for the first time, they gazed down upon the beautiful green meadows of the land that would become Kentucky. The mountain pass they had used came to be called the Cumberland Gap.

5

After years of searching, Daniel Boone and his companions found a trail through the Appalachian Mountains.

Boone crossed through the Cumberland Gap many times over the next several years. In 1775, he was hired to widen the Warrior's Path so that settlers with wagons and animals could use it. Boone and a crew of forty men chopped down trees and cleared away the underbrush. In just a few months, the new road, now called the Wilderness Trail, was ready for use.

The first settlers to follow the Wilderness Trail into Kentucky were some of Boone's relatives and friends. They started a settlement called Boonesboro. They were quickly followed by hundreds, then thousands, of other pioneers searching for new, rich land south of the Ohio River.

While thousands of pioneers poured across the Wilderness Trail into Kentucky and neighboring Tennessee, thousands more came by way of the Ohio River. They floated downstream on

The flat bottoms of the flatboats made it easy for pioneers to travel through shallow waters.

their **flatboats** until they reached the land they hoped to settle. By 1792, Kentucky had enough people to become a state. Tennessee became a state just four years later.

During those same years, pioneers also moved into the land north of the Ohio River known as the Northwest **Territory**. Most of the pioneers settled along the Ohio River or near the streams that emptied into it. The Ohio River, and the Mississippi River too, became water highways for Westerners to transport their farm products to market.

Vocabulary

flatboat, n. a boat with a flat bottom that can travel easily in shallow water

territory, n. an area of land

Chapter 2
Exploring the Louisiana Territory

Unknown Territory In 1803, the United States gained the Louisiana Territory, a vast area of land between the Mississippi River and the Rocky Mountains. Strange as it may seem, the United States government purchased this territory from France with little knowledge of what it was actually getting.

The Big Question

How might Lewis and Clark's expedition and findings have helped the United States government?

Even though some hunters had ventured into the Louisiana Territory and traded with Native Americans, the United States government knew very little about the land between the Mississippi River and the Rocky Mountains.

Was the land good for farming? What kinds of plants grew there? What kinds of animals or even mythical beasts lived there? What about the Native Americans who lived there—would they welcome settlers? Could trading opportunities be developed with Native Americans? How high were the Rocky Mountains, and was there a way to cross them? Better yet, might the land possibly contain a way to reach the Pacific Ocean entirely by water—the long-dreamed of Northwest Passage?

The Expedition

President Thomas Jefferson was very interested in scientific discovery. He decided to send an expedition to find the answers to these and many other questions. Jefferson chose his twenty-nine-year-old private secretary, Meriwether Lewis, to lead the expedition. Lewis had also served as an army captain on the frontier, and he was an experienced explorer. Lewis asked a friend from his army days, William Clark, to lead the expedition with him. Both men were filled with the spirit of adventure. It was a good thing, too, for there was plenty of adventure—and danger—ahead of them.

The two expedition leaders prepared for the long journey. They hired strong men to make the trip with them. They bought large amounts of clothing, tools, and medical supplies. They also bought plenty of ammunition. Even though the explorers were bringing several tons of food, they would have to hunt for most of what they would eat. They would also have to protect themselves from any dangers.

Knowing they would be meeting and dealing with many groups of Native Americans, Lewis and Clark also put together a list of goods to trade and to give as gifts, including 2,800 fish hooks and 4,600 needles, as well as colored beads, silk ribbons, and mirrors.

Finally the Lewis and Clark expedition was ready to depart. On a clear morning in May 1804, the explorers—along with soldiers, several experienced frontiersmen, and three **interpreters** who spoke various Native American languages—climbed into their boats on the Missouri River near the town of St. Louis. They were also joined by

As the group set off, they knew that for the next two years, and maybe more, they would be on their own. The great adventure had begun.

fifteen other men who would travel with them part of the way. Together, the men began to paddle the boats upstream.

Several months later, the group reached what is now North Dakota, where they stopped to spend the winter in a Mandan village. The Mandan were used to housing the fur traders who came through the area. There the group used their time well, repairing their equipment, making six new canoes, and learning all they could from the Mandan people about the land and about the other Native American tribes they might meet along the way.

Sacagawea

Realizing they would need more people who understood Native American languages, Lewis and Clark added two new people to their company. One was a French Canadian trapper named Charbonneau (/shar*bah*noh/), who had lived among Native Americans for many years. The other was Charbonneau's sixteen-year-old wife, Sacagawea (/sak*uh*juh wee*uh/), who was expecting a child. Sacagawea had been kidnapped as a young girl. Now she lived with her husband and the Mandan.

With the arrival of spring, the expedition, which they called the "Corps of Discovery," set out once more. They paddled up the Missouri River in their new canoes. The exploring party was now smaller, for this was as far as the extra men from St. Louis would go. But the expedition had also added a new passenger: Sacagawea's baby boy.

In the summer of 1805, the explorers reached the source, or starting point, of the Missouri River, in present-day Montana. They were entering the country of the Shoshone—Sacagawea's original people.

Sacagawea and her baby boy traveled with the expedition.

One day, Lewis and several of his men met a group of sixty Shoshone. They were friendly toward the explorers and welcomed them.

Several days later, it was arranged that Sacagawea would meet with the Shoshone leader. When she did, she could hardly believe her eyes. The chief of the group was her very own brother! The brother and sister had a joyful reunion.

Later, with Sacagawea's help **translating**, Lewis traded goods with the Shoshone for horses that would help the explorers cross the Rocky Mountains.

Vocabulary

translate, v. to restate in another language

By mid-August, the Lewis and Clark party had made it to the Continental Divide. This is the line high in the Rockies from which all the rivers flow to the east on one side and to the west on the other. It was an exciting moment for the group. But dangerous rocky trails lay ahead as they began their climb down the western slopes.

In October, the men lowered their canoes into the waters of the Snake River. They paddled down the Snake River into the Columbia River until, in November 1805, they sighted the Pacific Ocean.

Imagine the thrill this group of explorers felt at the moment they first spotted the ocean! William Clark wrote in his journal entry for November 7, 1805, "Ocean in view! O! the joy. " No words could have possibly captured the excitement of that moment.

After months of travel, the Lewis and Clark expedition finally reached the Pacific Ocean.

The Return Trip

After a mild winter on the Pacific Coast, it was time to head home. Sacagawea, her husband, and their infant son left the group when it reached the Mandan village from which they had started. The rest of the explorers returned to St. Louis in September 1806.

From there, Meriwether Lewis continued on to Washington, D.C., to report to President Jefferson about this newest U.S. territory. Both Lewis and Clark had kept detailed accounts of the expedition and their findings. This information greatly helped the United States government.

The Lewis and Clark expedition traveled more than seven thousand miles in just under two-and-a-half years. They had crossed the North American continent from one side to the other.

Zebulon Pike

Lewis and Clark were the most famous American explorers of the West, but they were not the only ones. Another explorer was a U.S. Army officer named Zebulon Pike. In 1806, the same year that Lewis and Clark returned from their great journey, Pike set out toward the West from Missouri. Meeting the Arkansas River far upstream, he followed it toward its source in the Rocky Mountains. There he sighted the mountain named for him today, Pikes Peak, in present-day Colorado.

Chapter 3
Native Americans Resist

Fallen Timbers Some settlers moving west liked to say they were moving to "empty land." The land, however, was far from empty. Much of it was inhabited by Native Americans who had lived there for hundreds, even thousands, of years. With every new push westward by the pioneers, the resentment of the Native American inhabitants grew.

The Big Question

Why was it a struggle for Native Americans to hold onto their land?

As far as many settlers were concerned, no one lived on the land they intended to take.

From time to time, organized fighting broke out. In an attempt to protect their land, Native Americans attacked groups of pioneers traveling on the Wilderness Trail. They raided settlements in new states and territories. They fired arrows at settlers traveling on flatboats on the Ohio River. The settlers and U.S. Army troops attacked and killed Native Americans in return.

Many conflicts occurred, and many lives were lost. Native American nations in the Ohio Territory managed to win several victories against the U.S. Army. In particular, the Battle of the Wabash in 1791 brought about one of the worst defeats of the U.S. Army by Native Americans. For Native Americans, this was their biggest victory. However, they were unable to stop the constant flow of settlers. They were also unable to prevent the American government from passing laws that allowed people to settle on what was once Native American land.

In 1794, several Native American tribes were finally defeated at the Battle of Fallen Timbers near the present-day city of Toledo. They were forced to give up nearly all of Ohio and move farther west. As the Native Americans left the Ohio Territory, settlers poured in. Soon there were enough settlers living there for Ohio to become a state in 1803.

Before long, settlers began to push into the Indiana Territory, right next door. The governor of the Indiana Territory was William Henry Harrison, a man who would later become president of the United States.

Governor Harrison did not try to drive the Native Americans out by force. Instead, he pressured and tricked several of their chiefs into

During this period in history, Native Americans were forced to leave their homeland and move from place to place.

signing agreements. The chiefs gave up huge amounts of their lands in exchange for small amounts of money—sometimes as little as a half penny an **acre**.

Tecumseh

A Shawnee Indian chief named Tecumseh watched with rising anger as one piece of Native American land after another was handed over to settlers, Tecumseh had been fighting against settlement since boyhood, when his father was killed by settlers. He had seen the remains of Shawnee villages after army troops had destroyed them. He had tasted the bitterness of being forced to leave the tribe's lands in Ohio after its defeat at Fallen Timbers.

Now, in the Indiana Territory, he was determined to stop the loss of Native American land. "These lands are ours," he declared. "No one has the right to remove us because we are the first owners. The Great Spirit above has appointed this place for us, on which to light our fires, and here we will remain."

After learning of another Native American sale of land, Tecumseh exploded: "Sell a country! Why not sell the air, the clouds and the great sea, as well as the earth? Did not the Great Spirit make them all for the use of his children?" Unlike Americans, Native Americans did not believe that land could actually be *owned*.

But Tecumseh knew it would take more than words to stop the settlers from coming. He believed that uniting was the only way for Native Americans to do that.

Tecumseh spent several years traveling up and down the frontier, urging Native American nations to join together. A number of them did.

Meanwhile, Governor Harrison watched Tecumseh's successes with growing concern. In 1811, while Tecumseh was in the south urging more chiefs to join him, Harrison sent nine hundred American soldiers to the site of a Shawnee village on the Tippecanoe River. The soldiers camped near the Native American settlement. While Tecumseh was gone, his brother Tenskwatawa ordered the Shawnee to attack the American soldiers. Tenskwatawa told the Shawnee that the soldiers' bullets could not hurt them. It was a fatal mistake. The Shawnee attack began the Battle of Tippecanoe. Harrison's forces defeated the Shawnee and burned their village to the ground. Tecumseh returned to find his home in ruins. Worse still, the defeat at Tippecanoe weakened Tecumseh's efforts to get other Native American nations to unite with the Shawnee.

Revenge

Tecumseh promised revenge. For the next year, Native Americans in the Northwest Territories attacked settlers. When the United States went to war against Great Britain in 1812, Tecumseh joined with British

forces and led several Native American tribes into battle against the Americans. His anger toward the Americans knew no limit. "We gave them forest-clad mountains and valleys full of **game**," Tecumseh told the British general, "and in return what did they give our warriors and our women? Rum and trinkets and a grave."

In 1813, however, Tecumseh was killed. His dream of protecting Native American lands died, but other Native American leaders continued the fight.

Tecumseh (1768–1813), chief of the Shawnee

Chapter 4
Improvements in Transportation

Getting Around As America's population grew and spread out, one thing became clear: the United States needed to improve its transportation system.

The Big Question

What were the advantages of traveling by steamboat rather than by stagecoach?

Conestoga wagon

People traveled long distances by stagecoach. In addition to the stagecoach, a wagon, known as the Conestoga wagon, was widely used to carry goods long distances.

By 1800, some improvements had already taken place. Many of the roads that connected the growing cities and towns of the East were widened, allowing them to handle wagon traffic and horses. It was now possible to travel between the main towns by stagecoach.

The Stagecoach

The stagecoach got its name from the way it traveled—in stages. Every fifteen or twenty miles, the driver of the coach stopped at a station to change the team of horses for the next stage of the journey.

Although stagecoach travel was an improvement over travel on horseback, it was still an uncomfortable experience. Travelers began their trip very early in the morning. Sitting on hard wooden seats in a coach without springs, passengers felt every bump and hole in the unpaved roads. Male passengers learned not to dress in fancy clothes. When the wheels of the coach got stuck in mud, the men were expected to help lift the coach out.

When the sun went down and the stagecoach stopped at an **inn**, passengers could expect a poor meal and a terrible night's sleep.

> **Vocabulary**
>
> **inn,** n. a place where travelers can pay to eat and sleep

The roads were a challenge, and weather conditions caused problems for travelers.

Turnpikes

Another transportation improvement was the development of roads called turnpikes. Just before 1800, some people figured out that if they could build good roads, they could charge people for using them. Every ten miles or so, the road's owners would collect a toll, or fee. They did this by placing a pike, or pole, across the road. This prevented the travelers from passing until they paid the toll. That is how the turnpike got its name: when the toll was paid, the pike would be turned, allowing the traveler to pass.

Some of these turnpikes were actually paved with stone or gravel. Most, though, were just improved versions of the old dirt roads—a little smoother, a little wider, with the tree stumps in them a little lower. Depending on the season, the newer roads were just as dusty or muddy as the older ones. Most of the turnpikes ran between the cities in the East, where there were many users to pay the tolls. No turnpike ran very far west.

Unfortunately, none of these improvements answered the growing needs of people who were moving west. There were few roads wide enough for wagons. That meant pioneers still traveled mainly on foot, leading a horse or mule that carried their supplies.

Steamboats

Improved roads were a big help, but they were still a very slow and expensive way for Westerners to ship their farm products to market. Rivers provided a better way to do that. Most of the streams west of the Appalachian Mountains emptied into the Ohio River. The Ohio, in turn, emptied into the great Mississippi River. Many settlers chose to farm the land along these waterways. They could load their goods on flatboats and float them downstream all the way to the port of New Orleans. From there, their goods could be sent by ship around the world.

Though flatboats were helpful in sending goods downstream, they could not return upstream against the current without great human effort. Most farmers would break up their boats and sell

Flatboats could only move downstream.

them for **lumber** after selling their crops in New Orleans. They then returned north on horseback or on foot. Future president Abraham Lincoln took such a trip as a young man.

What people living in the region really needed was a way to easily travel upstream. American inventor Robert Fulton believed he knew how to make this happen. He built a boat, placed two large **paddle wheels** on its sides, and installed a steam engine. The power from the steam engine turned the paddle wheels, which worked like oars and pushed the boat through the water.

Fulton named his boat the *Clermont*. Others who saw this odd-looking boat laughed and called it a different name: *Fulton's Folly*. But Robert Fulton had the last laugh. In August 1807, the *Clermont* steamed up the Hudson River against the current. It made the 150-mile trip from New York City to Albany in only 32 hours. Fulton's steamboat made the trip in far less time than a horse-drawn wagon could, and it carried a much larger cargo. Not much later, steamboats made their appearance on the Ohio and Mississippi rivers, carrying passengers and goods up and down these water highways.

Robert Fulton's steamboat, the *Clermont*, made the trip from New York City to Albany much faster than a horse-drawn wagon could.

Chapter 5
Canals and Railroads

Connecting Waterways Though the steamboat was an important invention, it could not answer all the transportation needs of the growing nation. Steamboats could only travel

The Big Question

What drove the need for better forms of transportation?

where the rivers ran. This posed a problem for people settling in the area between the Appalachian Mountains and the Mississippi River, where the rivers run mainly north and south.

Anyone wishing to send goods east or west still had to rely on overland travel, which was slow, expensive, and often dangerous. Getting across the Appalachian Mountains posed an even bigger problem.

Other than the Cumberland Gap, there are only a few lowland areas that pass through the mountains. One such place is in the northern part of New York State. Rather than build a road there, however, DeWitt Clinton, who was the Mayor of New York City and the Lieutenant Governor of the State, had another idea. Why not build a canal—a waterway that would connect Lake Erie with the Hudson River?

Trading on the Erie Canal

Map labels

ATLANTIC OCEAN

Hudson River

Erie Canal

Albany

New York City

Buffalo

Lake Ontario

Lake Huron

Lake Erie

APPALACHIAN MOUNTAINS

Cumberland Gap

Tennessee River

Ohio River

Illinois River

Lake Michigan

Lake Superior

Mississippi River

New Orleans

Mississippi River

Arkansas River

Missouri River

ROCKY MOUNTAINS

Goods could be shipped more easily and more affordably by canal than by wagons on poor roads.

N
W E
S

Hard Work

A canal would allow farmers near the Great Lakes to ship their corn, wheat, and hogs to Albany by water. From Albany, the goods could be shipped down the Hudson River to New York City.

Clinton's proposal was breathtaking. Several canals had already been built in the United States. The longest, however, was only twenty-seven miles long. Clinton's canal, later called the Erie Canal, would be 363 miles long. That would make it the longest canal ever built in the United States!

The canal was a challenge to build without modern tools, such as chain saws, steam shovels, and bulldozers. Every tree along the route had to be cut down by hand. All of the dirt had to be dug by thousands of workers, one shovelful at a time.

Many people felt that the canal was an impossible task. Even Thomas Jefferson, who was always interested in new ideas, said that Clinton's idea was "little short of madness." Despite such opinions, work on the Erie Canal began in 1817. Eight years later, the job was finished. People came to celebrate.

Part of the celebration included a fleet of boats that sailed the length of the Erie Canal. The boats were pulled by mules walking on a path alongside the canal. The boats set out from Buffalo at the western end of the canal on October 26, 1825. Clinton, who was now the Governor of New York State, rode on the first boat with two red, white, and blue barrels filled with water from Lake Erie. The fleet arrived in New York Harbor eight days later. The

Building the Erie Canal was an incredible accomplishment.

governor dramatized the great accomplishment by dumping the barrels of fresh water from the Great Lakes into the salt water of the Atlantic Ocean.

The Erie Canal was an instant success. Goods that had previously cost one dollar to ship overland from Buffalo to New York City could now be sent for less than a dime—and in half the time. Increased trade caused Buffalo to grow from a small town into a large city. New York City became the largest city in the young nation.

Other states rushed to copy the success of New York with east-west canals of their own. Even though none was as successful as the Erie Canal, these canals also encouraged settlement in the West.

Railroads

Not long after the success of the canal systems, a greater improvement in transportation was introduced—the railroad. The world's first railroad was built in England in 1825. Three years later, the first railroad in the United States was built in Baltimore, Maryland. The whole railroad track was just thirteen miles long. A team of horses pulled the wooden coaches along the tracks, which were made of wood with a strip of iron on top.

In 1830, a young mechanic named Peter Cooper designed and built a steam engine to pull the train. This **locomotive**, as Cooper called it, could reach a speed of

> **Vocabulary**
> ....
> **locomotive**, n. a railroad engine

eighteen miles an hour. That was many times faster than a wagon or a canal boat.

However, a person needed a taste for adventure to ride on one of the early railroads. The passenger cars that rode on the rails were basically stagecoaches. Passengers could choose to sit

Early railroad travel could be very dangerous.

inside the coach. They also had the option to sit in a seat on the outside located on top of the railcar. Either way, passengers could expect to be showered with the sparks and cinders from the locomotive's smokestack. One passenger riding inside a coach pulled by a locomotive counted thirteen large holes burned in her dress on a trip of just a few miles. Of course, the trip was worse for passengers riding on top. Smoke from the locomotive blew in passengers' faces the entire journey. The coaches often jumped off the tracks. The steam engines had a nasty habit of blowing up. If the locomotive broke down, the male passengers had to get out and push the train to the next town.

In the 1840s, railroad companies started using passenger cars shaped like long boxes, with seats on each side and an aisle down the middle. That was a bit better for passengers, but not much. In the winter, the companies put a **stove** at the end of each long car for warmth. Unfortunately, the stoves helped very little. Passengers sitting near the hot stoves roasted, while those sitting anywhere near the middle of the car still froze. At some stops, young boys climbed on board with hot bricks to sell so passengers could warm their feet.

Despite all these discomforts, traveling by railroad quickly became a popular way to travel. In the 1830s and 1840s, hundreds of railroad companies sprang up. Nearly all of them were small companies, with tracks only forty or fifty miles long. At that time, there was no national railroad network. That meant each company decided for itself how far apart to set its tracks.

One might set the tracks five feet apart, another two inches wider, a third two inches narrower. That meant that each company's locomotives and cars could only roll on its own tracks.

Think of what this meant for passengers traveling a long distance. Every forty or fifty miles, when the train reached the end of one company's line, passengers had to get off and walk a few blocks to the next company's railroad line, with its wider or narrower tracks.

If a passenger was traveling from Albany to Buffalo in New York State, a distance of about 320 miles by train, they rode on seven different trains. The whole trip took a day and a half.

Still, a day and a half was a lot faster than traveling by canal boat. A canal boat could only move as fast as a mule could tow it—about four miles an hour. Also, water cannot flow uphill, so a canal required fairly level ground. A railroad could be built almost anywhere. Water in the northern canals would freeze in winter, whereas the railroad could be used year-round. With railroads, farmers could ship their products to market faster, from almost anywhere, at any time of the year. By the 1840s, railroads had become the most important form of transportation in the country.

Chapter 6
Land, Land, and More Land

Native Americans React Settlers applauded each new improvement in transportation. Settlers who wanted to move farther west could

The Big Question

What was Manifest Destiny?

do so more easily. Farm products could now get to market in the East more cheaply and quickly. For Native Americans, however, each new road, steamboat, canal, and railroad meant that they were closer to being pushed off their land.

Developments in transportation, and increased settlement, meant that Native Americans were forced to relocate.

Forced Migration

During the late 1700s and early 1800s, Native Americans who lived north of the Ohio River lost their lands. The War of 1812 weakened their ability to resist. By 1830, most Native Americans in the East had been forced to move west of the Mississippi.

Still, nearly one hundred tribes remained on land in the East that settlers wanted. It is important to note that some people did understand just how unfair the taking of Native American land was. After a bitter fight, **Congress** passed the Indian Removal Act in 1830, by only three votes. Afterwards, people sent petitions to Congress protesting the new law.

> **Vocabulary**
>
> **Congress,** n. the law-making branch of the American government that is made up of the House of Representatives and the Senate

The Indian Removal Act said that the Native Americans must leave their homes and move west of the Mississippi. They would make their new homes in an "Indian Territory" set aside for them in present-day Oklahoma. A few tribes, such as the Sauk and Fox in Illinois, resisted but ultimately lost the struggle.

Five Tribes

Knowing that fighting against the U.S. Army was a losing battle, five Native American tribes that lived in the southeastern United States decided on a different strategy. These five tribes—the Choctaw, Creek (or Muscogee), Cherokee, Chickasaw, and

Seminole—believed that their best chance to keep their land was to adopt the ways of the settlers. The five tribes learned to farm like the settlers and grew the same crops. They dressed like the settlers and built similar homes. Many members of the five tribes became Christians.

The Cherokee even developed a written language. This was the work of a Cherokee named Sequoyah. Sequoyah created a written symbol for each of the eighty-six syllables in the Cherokee's spoken language. It was "like catching a wild animal and taming it," he explained.

Sequoyah developed a way to write the Cherokee language.

Soon the Cherokee were building schools for their children. They started a weekly newspaper. They formed a government like that of the United States. They even wrote a constitution based on the U.S. Constitution. Unfortunately, the efforts of the five tribes did not stop settlers from arriving. When gold was discovered on Cherokee land in Georgia in 1828, their fate was sealed.

It made no difference that the Cherokee had made a **treaty** with the United States government in 1791. The treaty stated that the land belonged to the Cherokee. Some Americans, including the Supreme Court, members of Congress, and others agreed that the treaty should be honored. President Andrew Jackson, however, sided with Georgia and other states. He chose to break the treaty and sent the army to help remove the Cherokee.

Today it may be hard to imagine Native Americans being forced to leave their homes and land. One army soldier later wrote, "I saw the helpless Cherokees arrested and dragged from their homes, and driven by bayonet into the **stockades**. And in the chill of a drizzling rain on an October morning I saw them loaded like cattle or sheep into wagons and started toward the west."

The journey to Indian Territory took several months. Most of the Native Americans walked the whole way. They suffered from disease, hunger, and bitter cold. About fifteen thousand people started out on

> ## Vocabulary
>
> **treaty,** n. a formal agreement between two or more groups, especially countries
>
> **stockades,** n. enclosures or pens usually made from stakes or poles driven into the ground

Thousands of men, women, and children died on the journey to Indian Territory.

the long trek. Only eleven thousand arrived in Indian Territory alive. Native Americans called this journey *Nuna-da-ut-sun'y*, which means The Trail Where They Cried or The Trail of Tears.

Osceola and the Seminole

Of the five tribes, the Seminole held out against the U. S. Army the longest. The Seminole had originally lived in the southern part of present-day Georgia. When the British colonists in Georgia tried to enslave them in the mid-1700s, the Seminole fled south to Florida. Florida was owned by Spain at the time.

In 1821, the United States gained Florida from Spain. Within a few years, the government took measures to remove the Seminole and send them to Indian Territory.

One of the Seminole chiefs who fought against removal was Osceola [/ahs*ee*oh*luh/]. As a boy, Osceola and his mother had moved from present-day Alabama to Florida. He was determined not to be forced to move again.

Osceola and his warriors defeated troops from the U.S. Army in several battles. The army commander invited Osceola to meet to discuss peace, but it was a trick. When Osceola arrived, he was taken prisoner. Although he was not kept in a prison cell, he was not allowed to leave the army fort. After a few months, Osceola's health became poor, and he died.

The Seminole fought on bravely, but they were eventually defeated and sent to Indian Territory in the West. Only five hundred Seminole remained, hiding in the **swamps** and forested areas of Florida. They were often joined there by enslaved workers who had run away.

> **Vocabulary**
>
> **swamp**, n. a wet, marshy area where water collects

The Rapid Growth of a New Nation

During the 1770s, settlement in the American colonies spread from the Atlantic Coast to the Appalachian Mountains. That was already an area four or five times larger than Great Britain, and for only one-third the number of people.

In 1783, the United States won its independence from Great Britain and gained all the land between the Appalachian Mountains and the Mississippi River. This doubled the size of the new nation, which was now more than twice the size of Great Britain and France put together.

When in 1803, President Jefferson bought the Louisiana Territory from France, this doubled America's size once again and pushed its western boundary all the way to the Rocky Mountains. The new nation had grown almost as large as the continent of Europe, except for Russia.

By the 1820s and 1830s, some Americans were wondering about other parts of the North American continent. One area of interest was the huge area from Texas to California, located between the present-day Mexican border and the states of

The United States of America grew rapidly in a short amount of time.

Colorado and Utah. Another area of interest was the Oregon Country, the area north of California, between the Rocky Mountains and the Pacific Ocean.

Manifest Destiny

What caused the rapid expansion of the United States? One reason was the need for more **fertile** farmland. Roughly nine out of ten Americans made a living by farming.

Growing tobacco, as well as other crops, took up most of the land in the East. The population was also rapidly increasing.

But there was more to it than that. Some Americans believed that they had created a special nation unlike any other. In the United States, citizens chose their own government. In turn, the government respected and protected the rights of its citizens. By expanding their country's boundaries, Americans said, they would be "extending the area of freedom" and bringing the blessings of liberty to the people who would live there. Some believed that it was America's *Manifest Destiny* to expand to the Pacific Ocean. By that, they meant that it was obvious to all, or manifest, that America's march to the Pacific Ocean was fated to happen, or destiny. Sadly, at this point in history, this vision of freedom did not extend to Native Americans or African Americans.

Believing in the idea of Manifest Destiny, pioneers kept moving westward.

Manifest Destiny also affected countries that controlled land along the U.S. border. Mexico and Great Britain claimed most of the land in these border areas. They did not think that America's march to the Pacific was inevitable. In fact, they were determined to prevent it. As for the United States, its vision of freedom did not extend to those living on or near the southern border with Mexico.

Chapter 7
Texas Joins the Union

Mexican Independence In the early 1800s, the people of Mexico rebelled against Spain, which had ruled their country for nearly three hundred years. Mexico won its independence in 1821 and took over all the Spanish lands in North America, including Texas.

The Big Question

What was the main reason the Texans and the Mexicans went to war against each other?

In the early 1800s, hundreds of settlers moved to Texas.

At that time few Mexicans actually lived in Texas. The new government of Mexico wanted to build up the area, but it was unable to persuade many Mexicans to move there. When Stephen Austin, an American, offered to start a colony of American settlers in Texas in exchange for land, the Mexican government gladly accepted.

In the early 1820s, Austin brought three hundred settlers from the United States into Texas. Later, he brought several hundred more. Austin wrote that the land was "as good in every respect as a man could wish for; land all first rate." The Mexican government soon made a similar deal with other Americans, and like Stephen Austin, they too started colonies in Texas.

It wasn't long before the Mexican government realized it had made a big mistake. Before settling in Texas, the settlers had made a number of promises. They promised to adopt the **Roman Catholic religion** of Mexico and to become loyal Mexican citizens. They also promised to free any enslaved workers they brought to Texas. The American settlers did not keep any of these promises. Instead, they ignored some of Mexico's laws and asked for more self-government. Some even talked about making Texas independent from Mexico.

> **Vocabulary**
>
> **"Roman Catholic religion,"** (phrase) a form of Christianity led by the pope, whose headquarters are in Rome, Italy

In 1830, the Mexican government announced it would not allow any more Americans to settle in Texas. But it was too late. There were already more than sixteen thousand Americans living in Texas. That was far more than the five thousand Spanish-speaking

The Mexican government did not expect so many Americans to travel to Texas. Before long there were more American settlers in Texas than Mexicans.

Mexicans living there. And because it was easy to cross the border into Texas, more American settlers came every year, regardless of what the Mexican government said.

The Alamo

During the early 1830s, the Mexican government took measures to tighten its rule over Texas. They wanted the Texans to obey the laws of the country in which they lived. The Texans became angry. Fighting broke out between Texans and Mexican soldiers in a number of settlements. Texas leaders decided to form an army. To lead the army, they chose a one-time U.S. Army officer and former governor of Tennessee, Sam Houston.

To Mexico's new ruler, General Antonio López de Santa Anna, that was the last straw. Early in 1836, General Santa Anna led an army of four thousand soldiers toward the settlement of San Antonio. There he intended to crush the rebels.

San Antonio was defended by a small group of Texans under the command of seventeen-year-old William Travis. Travis and his men could have safely retreated from San Antonio. Instead, they decided to take shelter behind the thick walls of an abandoned Spanish **mission** known as the Alamo. It was a decision that would cost them their lives.

> **Vocabulary**
>
> **mission,** n. a settlement built for the purpose of converting Native Americans to Christianity

On February 23, 1836, Santa Anna gave the order to attack the Alamo. Day after day Mexican cannons pounded the mission. The Texan rebels returned the fire. After twelve days, however, the Texans' ammunition was nearly gone, and the men were exhausted. In the early hours on March 6, Mexican troops stormed the walls of the Alamo. Twice they were beaten back. Finally, however, the Mexican soldiers made it over and through the walls.

All of the Alamo's defenders were killed. Among them were famous pioneers Davy Crockett of Tennessee and Jim Bowie, after whom the Bowie hunting knife was named. Only the lives of seven women, children, and servants were spared.

THE LAST STAND AT THE ALAMO

The flag that floated over the ill-fated mission fortress The Alamo, at San Antonio, in 1836, was that of the Republic of Texas, then fighting for the right to self-government. Its design was that of the Mexican flag, with the eagle, serpent and cactus replaced by the date 1824. This indicated adherence to the Texas constitution of that date, overthrown by Santa Anna, who established a dictatorship. Besieged by 4,000 troops under Santa Anna, the little garrison of 183 Americans held out 12 days under constant bombardment.

1824

From the flat roof with its thick adobe walls the Texan sharpshooters directed a devastating fire in the defense described in the diary left by Davy Crockett, famed scout, hunter and Indian fighter whose career ended here. Finally the defenders were so weakened that, after two unsuccessful assaults, an entrance was made through sheer weight of numbers and the five lone survivors were slain. The slogan "Remember the Alamo" became a battle cry which led to Santa Anna's destruction and the ultimate victory of the Texans.

THE ALAMO FLAG

Texan rebels could not hold off Mexican troops at the Alamo.

Texas Gains Its Independence

By the time the Alamo fell, Texans had already declared their independence from Mexico. They formed their own country and called it the Republic of Texas. Their new flag had a broad stripe of white and another of red that ran from left to right. The left side featured a stripe of blue that ran from top to bottom. In the center of the blue stripe, the Texans placed a single white star. As a result, the new Republic of Texas came to be called the "Lone Star Republic."

But the Texans had only declared their independence. To actually win it, they had to defeat the Mexican army. In 1836, the odds of a Texan victory did not seem likely. Mexico was a country of millions of people. Texas barely had thirty thousand. How could the

The single star on the Texas flag led to the nickname "Lone Star Republic."

Republic of Texas hope to assemble an army large enough to fight off the Mexican army?

In fact, in the six weeks following the Alamo, General Sam Houston and the Texan army retreated again and again from the larger Mexican army. Santa Anna was confident he would catch up with Houston and defeat his men.

What Santa Anna did not realize, however, was that Houston was not simply avoiding battle. He was building up and training his small army.

On April 21, 1836, the Mexican army was camped near the banks of the San Jacinto (/san/juh*sihn*toh/) River, less than a mile away from Houston and his army. In those days, battles always began in the morning and ended at nightfall. At 3:30 p.m., believing there would be no fighting until the next day, General Santa Anna allowed his men to put down their guns and rest.

This was Sam Houston's chance to move on the Mexican force near the river. Houston knew that General Santa Anna would be surprised. At 4:00 p.m. Houston lifted his sword—the silent signal for his army of 783 men to move forward. The Texans moved out of the woods that had sheltered them and advanced quickly and silently through a meadow of tall grass.

About two hundred yards from the Mexican camp, they were spotted by Mexican guards. The Mexicans fired. Two Texan cannons quickly answered the fire. As General Houston shouted the warning, "Keep low men! Hold your fire!," the Texans rushed forward.

General Houston and his men caught the Mexican army off guard.

Twenty yards from the edge of the Mexican camp, Houston gave the order: "Kneel! Shoot low! Fire!" The Texans stopped and opened fire. Then Houston, riding high on horseback, waved his hat—the signal to advance. The Texans rushed forward, guns firing and knives drawn, shouting, "Remember the Alamo! Remember the Alamo!"

The Battle of San Jacinto was over in less than twenty minutes. Half of the Mexican army was killed during this surprise attack. The rest were captured. Nine Texans were killed and another twenty-three were wounded, including General Sam Houston, who took a bullet in the ankle.

The Texans captured Santa Anna at the end of the battle. They threatened to put him to death unless he signed an agreement promising to withdraw all Mexican troops from Texas and to accept Texan independence. Santa Anna signed the agreement and was released.

Texas Becomes a State

With the fighting over, Texans elected Sam Houston to be the first president of their new country. Houston and most other Texans actually wanted Texas to become a state in the United States. However, Texas allowed slavery, and many people in the United States, especially in the North, did not want any more states that allowed slavery.

Texas waited nine years before Congress agreed that it could become a state. In 1845, Texas became the twenty-eighth state.

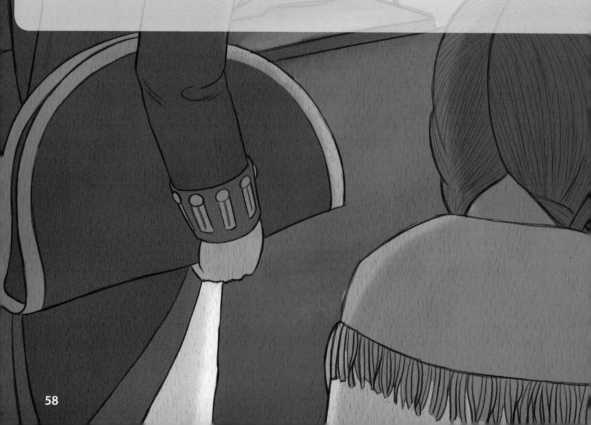

Chapter 8
Oregon

Oregon Country As with Texas, many Americans felt that gaining the Oregon Country was a part of Manifest Destiny. The Oregon Country was a large area between the Rocky Mountains and the Pacific Ocean. Its northern and southern borders were Alaska and California.

The Big Question

Why did settlers set off for Oregon, and what was different about the way they moved west along the Oregon Trail?

Trade, in particular the fur trade, was an important part of the economy that was being developed in Oregon.

Gaining the Oregon Country, however, turned out to be far more difficult for the United States than gaining Texas had been. It almost led to a war with Great Britain. In the end, the United States got only half of what it wanted.

Americans were interested in Oregon because of the animals that lived there. By 1800, beaver and otter furs were very valuable. They were used to make hats and fine coats on the East Coast and in Europe. New England merchants sent sailing ships around Cape Horn in South America and up to Oregon to trade with Native Americans for furs.

This journey to Oregon was thousands of miles long and very dangerous. Cape Horn, at the southernmost tip of South America, was known for its wild storms and rough water. Despite this fact, many merchants were willing to risk its perils for the fur trade.

The British also set up a fur-trading company in Oregon. Soon, with little regard for the Native Americans whose homes and hunting grounds they were invading, both Britain and the United States claimed the Oregon Country as their own. Few Americans or British actually lived there. As a result, the two countries agreed to delay the issue of ownership for a later time.

Mountain Men

While British ships continued to make the long and difficult journey to Oregon, American fur traders found a way to carry on the fur trade over land. In the Rocky Mountains there lived a number of hardy adventurers and fur trappers known as Mountain Men. The Mountain Men survived off the land and dressed in

buckskin clothing. They often lived alone, sleeping under the stars in good weather and in caves or lean-to huts in bad.

Vocabulary
....
buckskin, n. skin from a male deer

These Mountain Men became important in the story of Oregon. Although most could not read or write, they knew everything there was to know about the Rocky Mountains. It was Mountain Man Jed Smith who discovered South Pass, the best route through the Rocky Mountains for people headed to Oregon.

The Mountain Men were very rugged. They lived in the wilderness.

Some of these strong, tough Mountain Men were African Americans. One African American Mountain Man was Jim Beckwourth. He was born in Virginia, probably into an enslaved family, but he grew up in St. Louis as a free man. For eleven years he lived with the Crow nation, who called him Morning Star. Later in his life, he became an army scout and found a pass through the Sierra Nevada to California. Today this pass is called Beckwourth Pass.

Another Mountain Man, Jim Bridger, saved the lives of many travelers heading west. He provided supplies and information at his station, known as Fort Bridger. Bridger's first wife was the daughter of a chief of the Flathead nation.

Travelers did not begin heading for Oregon Country until the 1830s, when missionaries went there to convert Native Americans to Christianity. The missionaries failed to convert many Native Americans. But their reports about the beauty, mild climate, and rich farmland of Oregon encouraged some Easterners to **emigrate** there.

> **Vocabulary**
> ....
> **emigrate,** v. to leave one country to settle permanently in another

On the Oregon Trail

Soon a small trickle of farm families headed for Oregon. The first really large group of one thousand did not set out until 1843. That group was quickly followed by more. Although people had traveled by wagon before, these settlers traveled in wagon trains that sometimes stretched a mile or longer. A team of mules or oxen pulled each covered wagon in the slow-moving columns. Cows, **pack animals**, and even sheep moved alongside or behind wagons.

In the early spring, the families would gather in Independence, Missouri, and make final preparations for the six-month, two-thousand-mile trip. A month or so later, when enough grass had grown along the trail for their animals to feed on, they said their goodbyes and set out on the Oregon Trail.

For most of the men, women, and children who went, the trip to Oregon was the greatest adventure of their lives. The first part of

Wagon trains on the Oregon Trail snaked their way across the landscape.

The Oregon Trail started in Independence, Missouri.

the trail followed the shallow Platte River across the Great Plains. The grassland stretched as far as the eye could see.

On the trail, days began very early in the morning. Families ate breakfast, then did the morning chores: milking the cows, loading the tents and bedding into the wagons, hitching up the oxen. Then it was back on the trail for another fifteen or twenty miles before nightfall. That might seem like a lot of walking for one day, but people living in the 1800s were used to walking everywhere.

Not everyone got to ride inside the covered wagons. Only mothers, small children, and the sick and injured were allowed. The rest of the wagon was filled to the top with the family's belongings—everything they could bring to start a new life when they reached their destination. Most of the men rode on

At night, the settlers stopped to make camp.

horseback, guarding the wagon trains. Sometimes they rode off to hunt for food for that night's dinner. Older children walked, keeping the cattle moving along with the wagons.

At nightfall, the wagons pulled into a circle, with the animals inside the circle to keep them from wandering off. When things were going well, there would be dinner, perhaps a game of tag for the children, some singing around the campfire, and then an early bedtime to be ready for the next day.

Often, things did not go so well. Wagon wheels and axles broke; animals died; rainstorms turned the trail into mud. But the wagon train had to keep moving no matter what. It would have to get across the mountains before the snows arrived.

From the edge of the Great Plains, the trail to Oregon Country wound upward toward South Pass. After a short stop at Fort Bridger, the wagon train pushed on across the pass to the rugged western slopes of the mountains. This was the hardest part of the trip. Families sometimes had to throw away furniture and other heavy goods to lighten the load in their wagons. Sadly, sometimes precious belongings had to be left along the trail. The trail improved as it followed the Snake River and the Columbia River. Finally, the green meadows of the broad and beautiful Willamette Valley opened before the wagon train. The sight made all the hardships worthwhile.

Settlers knew where they were going, but they could not anticipate all of the problems along the way.

Oregon Country Is Divided

With Americans now pouring into the Oregon Country, the United States insisted that Great Britain should give up its claim to the area. Oregon—all of it, right up to the southern boundary of Alaska at 54° 40′ north **latitude**—must belong to America. Many Americans demanded, "Fifty-four forty or fight!"

The British, however, insisted that Oregon was theirs. For a time it looked like the two countries might go to war. But in 1846, they compromised. They agreed to divide the Oregon Country at 49° north latitude. The southern part, which included the present-day states of Oregon, Washington, Idaho, and parts of Montana, went to the United States. The northern part, which is presently part of western Canada, went to Great Britain. This decision benefited the British. The northern part of Oregon Country still had an abundance of animals that could be hunted for their fur.

Chapter 9
War with Mexico

Another War While the United States was able to avoid a war with Great Britain, war with another country was fast approaching, this time with a southern neighbor—Mexico.

The Big Question

Why did President Polk seek to gain land that belonged to Mexico?

Relations with Mexico had been getting worse for some time. President Polk strongly supported the expansion of U.S. territory along the southern border, and this desire threatened Mexico's claim to land they believed was theirs.

When Mexican troops crossed the Rio Grande onto what Americans believed was American soil, and attacked American troops, this was seen as an act of war. In May 1846, President Polk spoke to members of Congress about Mexico. He stated that Mexico had invaded America and shed American blood on American soil.

The president wanted Congress to declare war on Mexico. On May 13, 1846, Congress did just that. The United States and Mexico were now officially at war.

It is important to note that Mexico did not agree that they had invaded American land. They did not believe that the Rio Grande was

President James K. Polk (1795–1849)

the border between the two countries. Mexico claimed that the border was the Nueces (/noo*ay*says/) River, some 150 miles north of the Rio Grande. Mexico and the United States disagreed about ownership of the territory between the two rivers.

How had relations between Mexico and the United States become so bad? Why had war broken out between these two neighbors?

President Polk Looks to California

The reasons for the disagreement were based on the American desire to expand the size of the United States. President Polk had his eye on more than the land between the Rio Grande and the Nueces River. He also had his eye on California, which was under Mexican control.

When Mexico won its independence from Spain, it had gained all of the Spanish-owned land in North America, including California.

Early in the 1800s, a number of Americans arrived in California. Still, as late as the 1840s, there were fewer than one thousand Americans living there. There were ten times that many *Californios*, or Spanish-speaking people from Spain and Mexico. And there were many Native Americans.

However, President Polk knew that California had many fine harbors. These harbors could be excellent jumping-off points for trade with China and the rest of Asia. He also suspected that Great Britain had its eye on California and might take it if the United States did not.

President Polk also wanted New Mexico, the territory located between California and the western part of the United States. About 220,000 Spaniards and Mexicans lived there, but the territory had

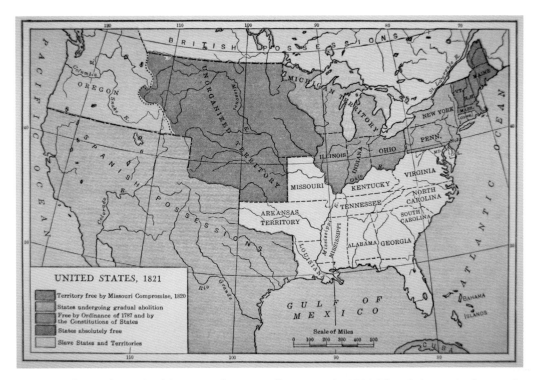

The map shows the United States and surrounding areas in 1821. The pink area in the north is Canada. The light green area in the southwest is Mexico. The other colored areas are regions of the United States. By the 1840s, many people from the United States had already moved into Mexican territory, which included Texas, New Mexico, and California.

very few Americans. However, Americans had long traded at the territory's only town, Santa Fe. Each spring, traders made the journey there from Independence, Missouri, along the Santa Fe Trail. In Santa Fe they traded their goods for silver, furs, and other frontier products.

The United States Declares War on Mexico

In 1846, President Polk offered to buy California and New Mexico from Mexico. The Mexican government refused to sell. So President Polk looked for another way to get this land. He ordered the American commander in Texas, General Zachary Taylor, to move troops across the Nueces River and to station them on the bank of the Rio Grande. This put American troops onto the disputed area of land between the two rivers. This was really an act of aggression by

America. President Polk expected the Mexican army to oppose this move—and they did! The outcome was war.

Some Americans Oppose the War

Not all Americans were pleased that their country had gone to war with Mexico.

One such person was a tall young man from Illinois serving his first term in Congress. His name was Abraham Lincoln. Lincoln challenged the president to point to the exact "spot" on "American soil" where American blood had been shed.

Many Northerners and abolitionists, or people who opposed slavery, were against the Mexican-American War. They thought it was a war to protect the interests of slave owners. They also feared any territory gained during the war would become a slave state.

In Concord, Massachusetts, a writer named Henry David Thoreau decided to protest the war by refusing to pay his taxes. He was put in jail overnight, but then his aunt paid the tax for him. While in jail, Thoreau was supposedly visited by his friend Ralph Waldo Emerson, a famous minister and author who also opposed the war with Mexico. "Henry!" exclaimed his friend. "Why are you here?"

"Waldo," replied Henry Thoreau, "Why are you *not* here?" Thoreau meant that when people believe their government is doing evil, as a matter of **conscience** they should peacefully refuse to join in that evil. This kind of behavior based on one's conscience is called civil disobedience.

> ### Vocabulary
> **conscience,** n. a sense or belief a person has that a certain action is right or wrong

The Bear Flag

People like Abraham Lincoln and Thoreau were in the minority, however. Most Americans supported the war, and tens of thousands of young men volunteered for the army.

In September 1846, the U.S. Army quickly struck against the Mexican forces. General Taylor marched his troops into northern Mexico. They captured the town of Monterey in a three-day battle with the trapped Mexican troops. Soon after, Taylor defeated Mexican troops at the Battle of Buena Vista.

A second, smaller American army marched into New Mexico and captured Santa Fe. From there the American army marched to California. When it arrived, it found that a handful of Americans living in Northern California had already overthrown Mexican rule.

GEN.ˡ TAYLOR, AT THE BATTLE OF BUENA VISTA.

Who, from a hill in the vicinity, saw, with exultation, his Spartan Band successfully repel the last charge of the terror-stricken Mexicans!

General Zachary Taylor, also known as Old Rough and Ready, led American troops to victory at the Battle of Buena Vista.

Because they raised a white flag with a cutout of a brown grizzly bear sewn on it, their uprising came to be called the Bear Flag Revolt. The Americans also set up their own government, which they called the Bear Flag Republic. Shortly after, American navy ships landed at Monterey, California. Raising the American flag, the naval commander proclaimed that California was now part of the United States.

The United States Grows Larger

Less than eight months after the war began, both New Mexico and California were in the hands of the United States. But there was still more fighting ahead in California.

The war finally ended after the American navy carried an American army to the shores of Mexico itself. There the army defeated the Mexicans in several battles. Six months later, the Americans entered the Mexican capital of Mexico City in triumph.

As a part of the peace treaty that ended the Mexican-American War in 1848, Mexico gave up almost all of the present-day American Southwest. California, the land that became the states of Nevada and Utah, most of what became the state of Arizona, and large parts of present-day Wyoming, New Mexico, and Colorado all became part of the United States. In return, the United States agreed to pay Mexico $15 million.

Five years later, the United States bought one more piece of land from Mexico. This strip of land forms the southern parts of present-day Arizona and New Mexico. It is known as the Gadsden Purchase.

Westward Expansion by 1853

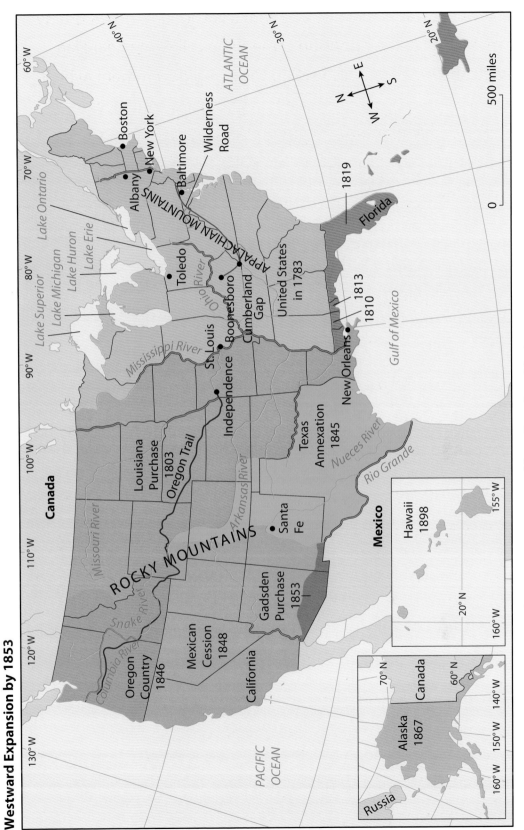

By 1853, the United States had spread from ocean to ocean and from Canada to Mexico.

Chapter 10
Settling the Far West

Reasons to Move West Most pioneers in America moved west in search of new land. However, two large groups who helped settle the Far West went for different reasons. One moved west to escape religious persecution. The other was drawn west by the promise of gold.

The Big Question

How do the experiences of the Mormons who moved west compare with those of the people who flocked to California?

The Mormons

Mormons were members of the Church of Jesus Christ of Latter-Day Saints. The church started in western New York in 1830. Most of its early members probably would have been content to remain right there if their neighbors had left them alone.

But many of their neighbors disliked the religious teachings of the new church. They viewed Mormon beliefs as a threat to a more traditional American way of life. The Mormons were forced to leave. That began a long trek for the Mormons. First, they moved to Ohio, then to Missouri, and then to Illinois. In each place they were unwelcome.

The Mormons moved west to escape mistreatment. Others moved west to look for gold.

When the Mormons moved to Illinois in the early 1840s, they felt they had finally found a home where they could **prosper** and grow. This feeling did not last. In 1844, a mob killed Joseph Smith, the founder of the Mormon religion and the leader of the Mormon community. More problems followed, and by 1846, angry mobs had chased the last of the Mormons out of Illinois.

Mormon leader Joseph Smith (1805–1844)

Their new leader, Brigham Young, led the Mormons westward in 1846. They searched for a place that would be far from everyone else, where they would be left alone to follow their religious beliefs. From Iowa, the group headed south until it picked up the Oregon Trail. They followed this trail until they reached South Pass. Then they turned south again.

In July 1847, Young and his exploring group of about 150 Mormons reached the top of a range of mountains near the Great Salt Lake, in present-day Utah. The area around the lake was very dry, and most people would not have chosen it as a place to farm. But Young knew that the soil was rich and that if the Mormons **irrigated** it and worked hard, they could succeed there.

> ### Vocabulary
>
> **prosper,** v. to be successful
>
> **irrigate,** v. to water crops by moving water from a well, a river, or a lake to a place where it does not rain enough to grow crops

In addition, the land at that time was not part of the United States. It belonged to Mexico. This meant the Mormons would not be subject to the laws of the United States. They would be left alone to make their own rules and to live as they wished. Looking down at the valley below, Young announced to his followers, "This is the place." Any man who wanted to settle there, said Young, would receive as much land as his family needed practically free of cost.

Within a few months, more than five hundred wagons and fifteen hundred of Young's followers arrived to make a new life for themselves. Working under the direction of church leaders, the Mormons prospered. Knowing that the salty water from Salt Lake was not suitable for farming, the leaders ordered that irrigation canals be dug between mountain streams and the **desert plain**. Soon, Mormon farmers were producing fine crops of wheat, vegetables, and other foods. Mormons also sold supplies to pioneers headed west to California.

> ### Vocabulary
>
> **"desert plain,"** (phrase) a large, flat area of land with limited rainfall and little vegetation

Before long, the Mormon population reached fifteen thousand. Most of the Mormon settlers lived in the City of the Saints,

Mormons built the City of the Saints, known today as Salt Lake City.

which later was called Salt Lake City. Others moved into the valleys of what would eventually become the states of Utah and Idaho.

Gold in California

Imagine what it must have been like to be James Marshall. John Sutter has hired you to build a **sawmill** for him on his land near the city of Sacramento, California. You get your crew started on the job and leave. On

a cold morning in January 1848, you have gone back to Sutter's land to see how the construction is going. The sawmill is located next to a stream, of course. It is the running water from the stream that will provide the power to run the mill. Standing next to the shallow stream, you look down and notice something shiny in the water.

How odd, you think. *I've never noticed that before.* You bend down and pick it up. It is a piece of yellow metal, about the size of a tiny stone. You look down again, and there's another one.

The discovery of gold near Sutter's Mill sparked the Gold Rush.

You pick up that one, too. Now your eyes begin to widen as you realize what you are holding. These little stones—they are gold! Pure gold!

You race over to Sutter's house to tell him the news. You both agree—the discovery must be kept a secret. If not, half the world will come to grab the gold for themselves.

Now, perhaps if you really had been James Marshall, you would have kept the secret. Perhaps John Sutter would have, too. And soon enough, you would have both been rich.

But that is not what happened. Historians do not know which man talked. Maybe other people just guessed from something that Sutter and Marshall said or did. In no time at all, the secret was out. "Gold has been found at Sutter's Mill!" The news spread through California. In the growing port city of San Francisco, people left their jobs, their ships, and their families as they rushed off to Sutter's land.

Within months, the news reached the entire United States and even Europe. People hurried to California from everywhere to claim their share of the wealth.

And Jim Marshall and John Sutter? They managed to get a little of it for themselves, but not much. Neither of them died a wealthy man.

California was far from where most people lived. Those traveling from the East could choose from three routes: two by sea and one by land. None of these were easy journeys. Travelers could expect several months at sea or several months overland by wagon.

Not one of those routes was fast. Not one was comfortable. But the lure of easy riches was so great that more than eighty thousand people journeyed to California in 1849 to seek their fortune. They became known as the "forty-niners."

Most forty-niners went to find gold, but some went to make a living by selling goods to the miners. Merchants became rich by buying **picks** and shovels back East, shipping them to California, and selling

them for ten or twenty times the original cost. A woman from Boston baked pies to sell to miners. She made $11,000 in one year! That was a huge amount of money in those days. A German immigrant named Levi Strauss made work pants for the miners. These "Levis" caught on, and Strauss made a small fortune.

As for the miners, the earliest to arrive quickly scooped up most of the gold that lay in the beds of shallow streams and on or near the surface of the earth. After that, it took a lot of digging and even more luck to find the precious yellow metal. A few miners did strike it rich. Most miners, though, barely found enough gold to make a living. In time, many of them gave up mining and raised crops or livestock instead. There would be other gold rushes in the American West, but by 1860, the great gold rush of California was just about over.

Many people became rich in California but not because they found gold.

Glossary

A

acre, n. an area of land that measures 4,840 square yards (19)

B

buckskin, n. skin from a male deer (61)

C

Congress, n. the law-making branch of the American government that is made up of the House of Representatives and the Senate (40)

conscience, n. a sense or belief a person has that a certain action is right or wrong (72)

D

"desert plain," (phrase) a large, flat area of land with limited rainfall and little vegetation (79)

E

emigrate, v. to leave one country to settle permanently in another (62)

F

fertile, adj. able to grow a large amount of crops (46)

flatboat, n. a boat with a flat bottom that can travel easily in shallow water (7)

frontier, n. where newly settled areas meet unsettled, but not necessarily uninhabited, areas (5)

G

game, n. animals that are hunted for sport or for food (21)

I

inn, n. a place where travelers can pay to eat and sleep (24)

interpreter, n. a person who translates from one language to another (11)

irrigate, v. to water crops by moving water from a well, a river, or a lake to a place where it does not rain enough to grow crops (78)

L

latitude, n. the distance between the equator and a place north or south of the equator; measured in degrees (67)

locomotive, n. a railroad engine (34)

lumber, n. wood that has been cut and is used for building (28)

M

mission, n. a settlement built for the purpose of converting Native Americans to Christianity (52)

P

pack animal, n. an animal, such as a horse or a mule, that is used to carry heavy loads (63)

paddle wheel, n. a large wheel with boards attached to it that help push a ship forward (28)

pick, n. a pointed tool used to chip away at rock or other hard surfaces (82)

pioneer, n. one of the first people to settle in a region (4)

prosper, v. to be successful (78)

R

"Roman Catholic religion," (phrase) a form of Christianity led by the pope, whose headquarters are in Rome, Italy (50)

S

sawmill, n. a place where logs are cut down to be used as lumber (80)

self-reliant, adj. needing no help from other people (4)

stockades, n. enclosures or pens usually made from stakes or poles driven into the ground (42)

stove, n. a device in which fuel is burned to generate heat, usually for cooking or warmth (36)

swamp, n. a wet, marshy area where water collects (44)

T

territory, n. an area of land (7)

translate, v. to restate in another language (13)

treaty, n. a formal agreement between two or more groups, especially countries (42)

CKHG™

Core Knowledge HISTORY AND GEOGRAPHY™

Series Editor-In-Chief

E.D. Hirsch, Jr.

Editorial Directors

Linda Bevilacqua and Rosie McCormick

Subject Matter Expert

J. Chris Arndt, PhD
Department of History, James Madison University

Tony Williams, Senior Teaching Fellow, Bill of Rights Institute

Illustration and Photo Credits